Prepared by the Department of the Environment
on behalf of the Welsh Office

Caernarvon Castle and Town Walls

Castell Caernarfon

GWYNEDD

A. J. TAYLOR   CBE, MA, D Litt, FBA, FSA, FR Hist S

Formerly Chief Inspector of Ancient Monuments and Historic Buildings

D1432520

LONDON: HER MAJESTY'S STATIONERY OFFICE
1953

ISBN 0 11 670101 3

Contents

Caernarvon from the north-east. Boydell's engraving, 1750

History and Periods of Building

. . . to Caernarvon, where I thought to have seen a Town and a Castle, or a Castle and a Town; but I saw both to be one, and one to be both; for indeed a man can hardly divide them in judgment or apprehension; and I have seen many gallant fabrics and fortifications, but for compactness and completeness of Caernarvon, I never yet saw a parallel. And it is by Art and Nature so fitted and seated, that it stands impregnable, and if it be well manned, victualled, and ammunitioned, it is invincible, except fraud or famine do assault, or conspire against it.
—JOHN TAYLOR, *A Short Relation of a Long Journey, Etc.* (1652)

Caernarvon before Edward I

CAERNARVON is one of the historic centres of Wales. Its remoter past was already enshrined in legend when, nearly seven hundred years ago, an English king chose it to be the seat of a new administration and gave it new fame as the cradle of a line of English princes. The Castle and Town Walls, built at that time and still in large part surviving, were the lineal successors of a Roman fortification raised a thousand years earlier, the ruins of which were then to be seen standing, where their foundations may yet be seen today, on the outskirts of the town astride the way to Beddgelert. Indeed it was from this site, excavated and as far as possible preserved in 1920–23, that Caernarvon took its name; for to the Welsh the Roman fort was "Y Gaer", distinguished from many another of its kind by the local suffix "yn Arfon". Arfon, the name of the cantred or tribal district lying along the Menai Strait, derived in turn from its situation "ar-Fon" – the land, that is to say, "over against Mon", the island of Mona or Anglesey. Another variant was Caer Segeint, for the fort's official title, the name by which the Romans themselves knew it, was Segontium, drawn from the ancient British word for the river Seiont, close to whose bank it stood, and whose waters, sheltered and tidal at this point, had much to do with its siting and carried much of its traffic. At a period probably even earlier than the coming of the Romans, whose first establishment at Segontium belonged to the years *c.* AD 75–80, there had been some kind of defended post on the rugged Twthill, lying on the other side of the Cadnant brook, the only visible evidence for which is the trace of a rock-cut ditch near its summit.

With the detailed history of Segontium as revealed by excavation we are not here concerned.[1] We may, however, refer briefly to one

---

[1]For a short account of Segontium and its position in the Roman occupation of Wales, *see* G. C. Boon, *Segontium Roman Fort* (Department of the Environment Official Handbook), 1963.

phase of it, as there are still to be seen in Caernarvon the remains of another monument which may be associated with that phase. Towards the end of the third century the Segontium garrison was withdrawn and the main fort left unoccupied until *c.* AD 350. Early in this period the whole defence system of the province of Britain was reorganised, and in the south-east the forts of the Saxon Shore, from Brancaster in Norfolk to Portchester in Hampshire, were established. In the west where sea raids from Ireland were the danger, similar measures of coast defence were needed, and there is reason to believe that it was at this time that smaller counterparts of the south-eastern forts were built to guard the Irish Channel. Parts of the walls of two of these structures are still standing to nearly their original height, the one at Holyhead and the other at Caernarvon. The "Lower Fort", as this latter is generally called, was set up on the cliff above the Seiont, between the river and the principal fort, and no doubt the Roman quay-side lay somewhere at its foot. The full length of its east and about half of its south wall remains, and today they enclose the backs of the row of houses known as Lon Bont Saint, in South Road.[1]

Little can be said with certainty or precision as to the status of Caernarvon in the six-and-a-half centuries that separate the evacuation of the Romans from the coming of the Normans. For the early part of the period history and legend are inextricably intertwined in the saga of the Mabinogion, in which the departed and no doubt poetically exaggerated glory of Segontium is the background for historical characters in heroic guise. Apart from the sheltering haven of the Seiont itself, one link and one link only, serves to connect the dimly seen realities of that almost vanished age with later and better known times. This is the site and dedication of Llanbeblig church, situated, not on the outskirts of medieval Caernarvon, but of Roman Segontium, yet continuing to this day as the mother church of the whole town. Peblig, whose name is derived from the Roman Publicius, is reputed to have been one of the sons of Magnus Maximus, Emperor of Gaul, Spain and Britain from 383 to 388, the Maxen Wledig of Welsh tradition; and in this church, and in the buildings, presumably going back to one of his foundation, which preceded it, Christian

---

[1]For descriptions of the Lower Fort, *see* R. E. M. Wheeler, *Segontium and the Roman Occupation of Wales* (Cymmrodorion Society, 1924), pp. 95–101, and Royal Commission on Ancient Monuments, *Caernarvonshire*, ii, p. 164.

worship has maintained continuity from the fifth century until our own time.

With the Norman Conquest, sealed by the coronation of William I at Westminster on Christmas Day 1066, we pass from a realm of obscurity to one of relatively well recorded fact. The new rulers of England lost little time in seeking to bring the regions of Wales under Anglo-Norman suzerainty, and already by 1073 a certain Robert, a kinsman of Hugh of Avranches, the first Norman earl of Chester, had established a castle, borough and mint at Rhuddlan and gained control of the northern coast lands up to the line of the River Conwy. By the time of the Domesday Survey (1086) this Robert of Rhuddlan, as he was called, had been granted a nominal lieutenancy over the whole of North Wales, but it was left to the earl himself, after Robert's death at Welsh hands in 1088, to carry effective Norman power into Gwynedd

7

and to establish, in or about the year 1090, castles at Aberlleiniog in Anglesey, at Caernarvon, and at a site in Meirionydd not yet certainly identified.

Earl Hugh placed his castle at Caernarvon at the water's edge, on the peninsula formed by the estuary of the Seiont, the Menai Strait and the Cadnant brook. So far as it is known, this ground had not been previously fortified, and to him thus belongs the credit of choosing the position which was to be ennobled, two hundred years later, by the genius of Edward the First and his architect, with the magnificent array of towers and turrets which are Caernarvon's abiding glory. The eleventh-century castle was of the motte-and-bailey type, with steep earthen banks and heavy timber palisading. Its dominant feature, a circular mound of the pattern made familiar by such striking examples as those at Windsor, Shrewsbury or Cardiff, was later actually incorporated within the upper or eastern ward of the Edwardian building, there to survive in a modified form until after 1870. The position occupied by Earl Hugh's bailey is less certain; probably it lay to the northeast of the motte and included part of the open ground later known as the Prince's garden and now represented by Castle Square. As to the buildings associated with the earthworks, it is likely that there would have been a tower on the mound and that at first this would have been a timber structure; but it would be unwise to assume that it necessarily remained so through the succeeding two centuries, so that no stone buildings were erected by the Welsh princes, who, having recovered their losses in Gwynedd by 1115, retained possession of Caernarvon until the final collapse of native power in 1283. Indeed the analogy of such other Welsh fortified residences as the castles of Dolbadarn or Dolwyddelan, to name only two examples, would suggest the contrary. We know from documents dated there that Llywelyn the Great (1173–1240) sometimes resided at Caernarvon, as likewise did Llywelyn ap Gruffydd (d. 1282) later in the thirteenth century. We know also that around this dwelling of the princes there lay a typical Welsh royal *maenor*, whose territory included most of Llanbeblig, with other neighbouring hamlets, and whose townsmen, endowed with agricultural holdings in the surrounding fields, and trading through their river port, were the predecessors of the privileged English burgesses soon to be settled on their lands under charter from King Edward I.

The building of the town and castle, 1283 to c. 1330

In the year 1283 we enter on a new era. From this date onwards the survival of contemporary records, though but a fraction of those originally kept, enables us to follow the growth of the buildings we now see and to reconstruct the different stages of the work with reasonable confidence. Since Palm Sunday (22 March) 1282, there had been war, for the second time in five years, between Edward, King of England, and Llywelyn, Prince of Wales. In December 1282, Llywelyn had been killed, and then on 18 January the English capture of Dolwyddelan castle, the key to Snowdonia and hub of its communications, opened the way through the Conwy Valley, the Llanberis Pass and the Vale of Ffestiniog, to Conwy, Caernarvon and Harlech. The king himself arrived at Conwy on or about 14 March, and the construction of Conwy castle was begun immediately. The fall of Castell y Bere (north-west of Towyn) on 25 April secured the southern flank of the English advance, while the capture of Dolbadarn, probably sometime in May, denied Llywelyn's brother, David, his last remaining stronghold. Within a few weeks the works begun at Conwy in March were being parallelled at Caernarvon and Harlech, and, in the years that followed, this great trio of castles, conceived on a scale which overshadowed even the might of those so recently built at Flint, Rhuddlan and Aberystwyth, rose with astonishing speed to embrace and grip the intractable heart of northern Wales.

Here we are only concerned with Caernarvon. From the beginning, the castle, the town with its wall and gates, and the quay to which most of the heavy building materials were brought by coastal shipping, were pushed forward as parts of a single operation, and the building of one was to some extent dependent on the building of the others. All, so far as we can now judge, were begun more or less simultaneously in the summer of 1283; for in the earliest weeks the documents refer repeatedly to construction having been started on both the castle and the town. The very first entry (24 June) mentions work on the new castle ditch, which would separate the castle from the streets and houses to the north. Next, as was done during the building of other North Wales castles, a *bretagium* or barricade was erected to fence in and protect the site of the new works. Great quantities of timber were shipped from Conwy, Rhuddlan and Liverpool, and use was also made of wood from the pontoon bridge by which, not many months earlier, an ill-starred English force had crossed from Anglesey, only to be annihilated on the Bangor shore. Diggers in their hundreds, directed by a Master Manasser, an expert from Vaucouleurs in Champagne who settled in Caernarvon and later held municipal office there, besides excavating the castle moat, levelled platforms in the rock and cut the great foundation trenches required for walls some of which at their base are nearly 20ft thick. Where houses of the old Welsh township lay in the way, they were demolished and their timber impounded, compensation not being paid till three years later. On the site of the future castle substantial timber-framed apartments were erected for the accommodation of the king and queen, who arrived from Conwy on 11 or 12 July and stayed for more than a month before continuing their journey through Bala, Ruthin and Chester to Shrewsbury and Acton Burnell. Preparatory work went on during the winter, and by the time Edward and Eleanor came again to Caernarvon in April 1284 much progress must have been made. On this second visit the king and queen almost certainly lodged in the buildings prepared for them the year before, and it must have been in these that their son, Prince Edward, was born. By now the new moat was ready to receive its turf revetment, lime was being supplied to the castle, and stone was being ferried across from Anglesey. In this spring and summer of 1284 much of the building we now see must have begun to take visible shape; the construction of the town walls was also progressing, and by the end of the following season (1285) it was probably substantially complete. Very heavy expenditure in the 1286 building season shows that work on the castle was then still continuing unabated. In 1287 the high proportion of expenditure assigned to "task" or piece work is an indication that the chief emphasis was by that time no longer on the mass employment of masons and labourers which prevails when main structures are in building, but rather on the "fitting out" and on the particular jobs more easily handled by smaller groups of craftsmen. In the 1288 season works expenditure, though still appreciable, was not a tenth of what it had been. In the three following seasons it was negligible, and after 1292 the accounts cease altogether. By this date there had been spent on the castle, town walls and related works a sum totalling approximately £12,000, which, if we use a multiple of 100 based on comparative wage rates, is equivalent to £1,200,000 in modern money. This is a vast sum, but is not disproportionate to the achievement it represents. The town walls were probably finished. The whole external southern façade and east end of the castle, from the Eagle Tower round to the North-east Tower,

had been built to a good height, completing the total enclosure formed by castle and town wall together.[1] We cannot be more precise. For while it is known that the top floors and turrets of the Eagle Tower were additions to the lower storeys and not finally completed till the year 1317, neither the records nor the structures themselves afford such

---

[1]The evidence upon which this reading of the building is based is set out in *Antiquity*, XXVI (1952), pp. 25–34, where reasons are given for rejecting the view formerly held that the castle was built in three distinct sections each at a separate period of time. For the figure of £12,000, *see The History of the King's Works* (London, 1963), i, pp. 372–7. As to the multiple of 100, the building craftsman of *c.* 1300 received on the average a wage of 4d for working an average 10-hour day. The prevailing rate for building tradesmen in 1952 was 3s 4d an hour i.e. 400d for a 10-hour day. Overtime and other restrictive practices which apply today tend if anything to increase relative costs, and in this respect the rough modern equivalents here given are probably on the low side. These broad figures of comparison held good in 1952 when this handbook was first written. At the present time no revised multiple could be very close for long so the 1952 approximation is retained.

definite information about the other southern and eastern towers, some or all of which may possibly not have received at any rate their turrets and perhaps some of the chapels adjoined to their inner sides until after the resumption of building in 1296. This second stage in the work will be referred to shortly. Construction of the north side of the castle, which was within the covering protection of the walled town and therefore not exposed to direct attack, would not at first have seemed an urgent matter. Moreover the castle was protected on this side by the great ditch hewn out at the very commencement of the work in 1283–84, a more formidable obstacle than might appear from the straitened form in which we see it today. Consequently, as we can deduce from a contemporary record, the northern curtains had only been built to a height varying between 12ft and 24ft above the bottom of the ditch by the time work was about to be taken up again in the spring of 1296. By then the northern towers had also certainly been begun, but we do not know to what height they had been carried.

Meanwhile Caernarvon's future status had been determined by events which followed closely upon each other in 1284. One was the promulgation at Rhuddlan, in March, of the Statute which, *inter alia*, established the three shires of North Wales as an administrative unit, with Caernarvon as the county town of one of them, and the centre of government for the whole. The other was the birth within the castle precincts, on 25 April, of a prince who was to become, on his ten-year-old brother Alfonso's death four months later, the king's eldest surviving son. It was not, however, until 1301 that Edward of Caernarvon, as he was named from his birthplace, was formally created Prince of Wales and endowed with the rule and revenues of all the Crown's Welsh lands; from that date the title has always been accorded to the eldest son of the reigning monarch. Whether or not one of the intentions of the formal act of 1301 was to give legal effect to an earlier nomination, traditionally supposed to have been made to the Welsh nobility in the year of his birth, of a prince "that was borne in Wales and could speake never a word of English", will perhaps never be known. The story is one that cannot be traced in writing until three hundred years later, but it is not inherently improbable and may well embody a genuine tradition. At all events, no episode is more widely associated with Caernarvon in popular thought. In 1911, when processes undreamt of in 1300 had placed among the king's chief ministers at Westminster a Welshman elected to represent the Caernarvon

Boroughs, the castle became for the first time the scene of a ceremonial Royal Investiture which clothed the forms and memories of the past in modern pageantry, and thereby furthered in this respect Caernarvon's claims to primacy among the towns of Wales. In 1963 Her Majesty the Queen conferred upon it the title and status of a Royal Borough.

When the first English Prince of Wales was a boy of ten, and the building of the castle had reached the stage described above, the Welsh, led by Madoc ap Llywelyn, a cousin of the last Welsh prince, rose in general revolt. Caernarvon, alike the symbol and centre of the new order, was overrun, and the sheriff, one of the officers established by the Statute of 1284, was assassinated. Very heavy damage was done to the new town wall, and once this barrier had been passed only the wooden *bretagium* and the moat would hinder the insurgents from swarming into the hated castle across the top of its embryo northern defences. A variety of evidence suggests that this is what they did and that, once they were inside, everything combustible was put to the flame, perhaps among the rest those timbered apartments that had witnessed young Edward's birth and may till then still have been standing within the castle ward. Our own narrative itself suffers for the loss of records then destroyed.

By the following summer vigorous English reaction recovered what had been lost, and orders were given for putting the town in a state of defence again not later than 11 November 1295. This involved work at high pressure, and two months before the target date the rebuilding of the town walls had been completed at a cost of £1,195 (say £120,000 in 1952 figures). This sum, nearly half the walls' original recorded cost, shows that in places the damage must have amounted to complete destruction, thus confirming that contemporary references to the *muri ville per Wallenses prostrati* (thrown down) were not exaggerated. Next, the repair of the castle damage was taken in hand and preparations made to resume work on a major scale in the following February on the unfinished parts of the building. Events had demonstrated that the completion of its townward side was, after all, a vital task, and a document has survived suggesting that this was the section with which it was intended to proceed. Between July 1295 and the end of 1301 nearly £4,500 was expended on the castle works, adding a round half-million to the rough modern totals already recorded. Probably by the latter date the building up of the four lengths of curtain wall linking the Eagle and the North-east Towers had made good progress, and it is

CC—C

fair to presume that at least the outer faces of the intervening towers would also by this time have been carried up to an equivalent height. The vaulted passage of the King's Gate, with its most elaborate provision for the detection, control and discomfiture of unauthorised entrants, and the arrow-slits grouped to give maximum fire-power from the curtain walls to the east, are of this period and later and reflect the sense of insecurity left by the recent disaster.

In 1301–02 orders were given to rebuild in stone the wooden bridge by which, prior to 1294, the main gate of the town had been approached across the Cadnant (see page 48). Then, between November 1301 and September 1304, there is a gap in the accounts. This may mean that building at the castle had been largely brought to a standstill by the transfer of all available labour to the war in Scotland. Walter of Hereford, the architect who had had charge of the works since 1295, was certainly in Scotland during the years in question, and he and his staff can be traced at Perth, where they were sent to build a town wall, and at Stirling, where they were employed on the seige works, in the first half of 1304. But as the Scottish commitment became less urgent, it was possible to take up once again the unfinished buildings at Caernarvon, to whose seemly completion point had now been added by the formal bestowal of the principality upon the king's heir.

The works were resumed in the autumn of 1304 and we know that approximately £700 was spent on them in each of the next two years. Expenditure of this order allowed the employment of 70 to 100 men in the winter months and 150 to 200 in the summer. Though details are lacking, there is no reason to suppose that progresss was not maintained at something like this level through the three following years also. From 1309 until 1330, and very possibly for a few years longer, building went steadily on, but on nothing like the scale reached in the 1280s and after Madoc's revolt. The records may not be quite complete, but such as they are they show that payments for the twenty-six years from 1304 to 1330 amounted to rather less than £7,500, an average of under £300 a year compared with over £2,000 a year in the period 1284–87. Nor was all of this absorbed by the castle. We know, for example, that between 1309 and 1312 the towers and wall-walks of the town walls were being extensively repaired. Again, in 1316, we read of the rebuilding in stone of the timber quay which the Welsh had burnt in 1294, and of the repairs to the town bridge in 1320. Moreover, at the castle itself some of the work may have consisted in replacing or repairing timber floors and roofs which had perished in or as a result of the damage done by the revolt. Proportionately to the whole building, therefore, we should expect to assign relatively little new construction to these final years, and there are documents which help us to say what it was. In 1316 the timber-framed "Hall of Llywelyn", part of the last Welsh prince's former residence at Conwy, was dismantled and shipped to Caernarvon, where it was re-erected within the castle. In 1317 the Eagle Tower was nearing completion, and a stone eagle was being affixed to it. There is evidence in the building itself that in the 1280s this tower had been left with a temporary roof at what was ultimately the level of its top floor. The addition of its fourth storey, battlements and triple turrets – all no doubt provided for in the original plans – was a major task, and must have accounted for a high proportion of the later expenditure. The fact that external string courses and moulded battlements are found on the upper part of the Eagle Tower alone, serves to emphasise the likelihood that the external faces of the main southern and eastern towers had *per contra* been carried up to their full height at an earlier date, i.e. prior to 1294. A band of decorative Aberpwll stone, consisting of only a single course of masonry, may mark the upper limit of the first work on the Eagle Tower; on all the other outward-facing towers, from the Queen's round to the North-east, and on the intervening curtains, the corresponding band is of four courses, and probably that on the Eagle Tower would have been of four courses too, if work had not been halted for an appreciable interval when it reached that level. Another piece of work belonging to this period, also marked by an external string course in contrast to the earlier banding, is the upper part of the curtain wall linking the Eagle and the Queen's Towers. A third is the upper portion of the King's Gate, where, as we learn from the accounts, the statue of Edward of Caernarvon (by this time King Edward II) was being erected in 1321. In the same year oak beams 32ft long, from the woods in the Conwy Valley, were being obtained to floor the hall above the gate. Probably one of the last works undertaken was the rearward extension of the western gate tower; this was apparently designed to be the first instalment of a scheme which, if completed, would virtually have trebled the defences of the entrance, with subsidiary gates and portcullises opening east and west towards the respective baileys from a central octagonal space. It can be seen to be an addition to the main gate structure, which at courtyard level itself belongs to a date after 1295;

whether more of it was built than now remains is impossible to say. In relating what we see to what we know was spent, we have to make allowances for the loss of much wood, iron and lead work, and perhaps also of entire ranges of building which were certainly intended and may have been erected, if only in temporary form, against the curtain walls on either side of the Well Tower.

Speaking broadly, by 1330, when regular building payments cease to be recorded, the structure of the castle had been carried to much the state in which we now see it, such subsequent works as we have record of being only of a minor character. The total expenditure from 1283 onwards had been from £20,000 to £25,000; using the same multiple as before, this represents between £2 and 2½ millions in terms of 1952 figures, its outlay being spread over nearly fifty years. It includes, as has already been indicated, the cost not only of the castle itself, but also of the town wall with its gates, towers and multi-arched bridge approach, the quay and other works, and in addition to all this the extensive reparations made necessary by the damage of Madoc's rising and of an accidental fire which swept the town in 1304. Even so, much that was planned in the castle was never undertaken. The Queen's Gate, the outer façade of which was almost certainly completed in the 1280s, was left unfinished at the back, as may still be seen from the toothing of its ragged wall-ends. Similar toothing on the North-east and Granary Towers is an indication of unbuilt wings, two storeys high, against the adjacent curtain walls. A massive foundation, projecting inwards from the wall between the Black and Chamberlain Towers suggests that it was proposed to enclose this side of the Norman mound with a wall which would probably have connected with the intended buildings at the back of the King's Gate. How the thirteenth-century builders would have dealt with the mound itself is matter for conjecture; the heavy stone revetment with which they encased and contained it would have enabled it to bear the weight of heavy masonry.[1]

Later history

The growth of the castle has been traced in some detail, not only because of the striking appearance of its buildings and their great intrin-

---

[1]Some vaults were reported to have been found when a cutting was made in the mound in 1847.

sic interest for all who see them, but also because of the importance of establishing as accurately as possible the dating of the different parts of one of the noblest examples of medieval military architecture in Britain. Space does not allow the same attention to be given to its subsequent history.

For two hundred years the political arrangements established by the Statute of Wales (1284) remained in force, and walled towns such as Caernarvon continued to be closed to all but English burgesses. The accession to the English throne, in 1485, in the person of Henry Tudor, of a king of Welsh lineage, opened the way to concessions in this respect to the Welsh-speaking population, and led fifty years later to a measure of assimilation of the governmental system of Wales to that of England. Until the time of these changes, the castle was more or less continuously maintained and garrisoned, and successfully withstood sieges by Owain Glyn-dŵr and his French allies in 1403 and 1404. Town and castle together formed the effective capital of North Wales, providing at once a safe residence for government officials and a centre for their activities. "In those dayes," wrote Sir John Wynn of conditions in the mid-fifteenth-century, "Caern'von flowrished aswell by trade of marchandise as also for that the kings exchequer Chauncerie and comon lawe courts for all northwales was there contynuallie resideinge, the waye to london and to the marches litle frequented wherebye Civilitie and learninge flowrished in that towne, soe as they were called the lawiers of Caern'von, the marchants of Bewmares, and the gent of Conway. I heard divers of Judgement and learned in the lawes to report that the records of the kings Courts, kept in Caern'von in those dayes were as orderlye and as formallie kept as those in Westminster. Thither did his foster father send my great-grandfather to scoole, where he learnt the englishe tongue, to reade, to writte, and to understand lattin, a matter of great moment in those dayes."

Tudor rule, by softening old hostilities and promoting peaceful intercourse with England, diminished the need for English castles in Wales. From the sixteenth century onwards, therefore, these great buildings were increasingly neglected, and in 1538 Caernarvon, with the rest, was reported as "moche ruynous and ferre in decaye for lakke of tymely reparacions". The walls, then as now, were "exceeding good", but in several of the towers roofs whose lead work had had no major renewal for centuries had brought their rotting timbers crashing through the floors below. In 1620 only the Eagle Tower and the King's

Gate were still roofed and leaded, the ground-floor rooms on either side of the latter having long been used as county prisons, the one for felons and the other for debtors; as for the buildings within the castle, they were, "all quite faln down to the ground and the Tymber and the rest of the materialls as Iron and Glasse carried away and nothing left that (is) valiable".

Such was the condition of a building which, in the Civil War, was once more garrisoned for the king and thrice beseiged. But to external appearance little was amiss, and after the war, as before it, a sensitive observer could not but be enraptured by the strength and perfection of the fortifications.[1] There were others, however, who only saw them as a source of trouble, and in 1660 the government gave orders for the castle and town walls to be dismantled and demolished at the expense of the county, the cost to be defrayed as far as possible from the sale of the materials. Local authority readily agreed, "conceiving it to be for the great advantage of ourselves and posterity to have the Castle of Carnarvon and the strengthes thereof demolished". Perhaps the "strengthes thereof" prevailed, for demolition, if indeed it was ever started, cannot have proceeded far, and posterity is still happily free to decide whether the destruction of a monument of a grandeur unsurpassed in Wales if not in Britain would after all have been so greatly to its advantage.

Caernarvon having thus escaped disaster, the eighteenth-century engravers such as the brothers Buck (1742) and John Boydell of Hawarden (1750), were able to take pleasure in depicting a town and castle whose site, character and setting had in essentials scarcely altered from their foundation. The change to modern conditions did not set in till the very end of the century. New roads, the first since Roman days, were built, and the North Wales slate industry was then expanding to serve both home and overseas markets. Hitherto unknown prosperity came to the port and in 1827–28 the brothers Robert and George Stephenson constructed a narrow-gauge railway to bring to the new "slate quay" below the castle the products of the Gloddfarlon quarries at Nantlle, ten miles away. The slate trade, more than any other single factor, accounted for a rise in Caernarvon's population from less than 4,000 in 1801 to more than 10,000 in 1851. In 1843 a local ship-owner, with offices in the High Street, was even inviting emigrants to sail direct from Caernarvon to New York in

---

[1]Cf. the quotation on page 5.

his fast 600-ton sailing barque *Hindoo*, "with a ballast of slates". In 1852 the town was connected by standard-gauge railway to the main London, Chester and Holyhead line; this meant further expansion of the slate trade, with slates carried quickly and cheaply to places inaccessible to water-borne traffic, while for Caernarvon itself the new means of communication marked the end of the era of isolation and self-sufficiency.

It was at this time of growing contact with a world beyond the limits of North Wales that the castle began to be rescued from the neglect of centuries, and a programme of repairs undertaken at government expense. The work thus begun was pursued with vigour in the last thirty years of the nineteenth century under the direction of the deputy-constable, Sir Llewelyn Turner (1823–1903). He renewed the stone steps and newels in several of the towers, restored battlements, repaired the Chamberlain Tower, rebuilt the top of the Well Tower, floored and roofed the Queen's Tower and, in the teeth of local opposition, cleared out the northern moat and removed a clutter of unsightly encroachments from against the outer walls.

Turner's new ashlar work is readily distinguishable by the buff colour and fine grain of the material employed, a sandstone from the neighbourhood of Mostyn in Flintshire. The appearance of the castle today owes much to his vision and pertinacity.

In 1908 control of the castle, which has at no time been alienated by the Crown, was transferred from the Office of Woods and Forests (which had become the responsible Department in 1832) to HM Office of Works, since when it has been maintained as a historic building under the supervision of the Ancient Monuments Branch of that Office and its successor the Department of the Environment. Further repairs were undertaken in connection with the Investiture ceremony in 1911, and the massive ceilings in the principal towers, following the evidence of those that had been there originally, are of this period. The Town Walls, having become annexed to and for much of their length obscured by the various properties built against them (for the most part in the early years of the nineteenth century), have also been opened up again and treated as a monument deserving the same care and appreciation as the castle. Their clearance was completed in 1963.

The purpose of the town and castle

In tracing the history of Caernarvon, certain topics of special interest have been omitted as not fitting into the ordinary course of the narrative. It will be convenient to refer to them here.

When Edward I began to build the walled town in 1283, and issued its charter of privileges in the following year, his principal object was to create a nucleus of English influence which could adapt a place famous in Welsh story and with great natural advantages to conditions brought about by the success of his armies. An early draft of the Statute of Wales shows that even before it was decided to form a county of Caernarvonshire, Caernarvon had been selected as the administrative centre for the lands subsequently grouped in the new shires of Caernarvon, Anglesey and Merioneth. The Justiciar and Chamberlain of North Wales, established to administer the judicial and financial systems of the principality thus annexed to the English crown, accordingly had their offices in Caernarvon; there the courts were held for the three shires, and there the justiciar had his chief official residence. Within the county organisation, the sheriff, the coroners and other local officers were based there. The new town provided quarters and protection for all these officials, their deputies, clerks and assistants; for the builders and craftsmen who worked on the castle; and for a small maritime and mercantile community who maintained contact with the other English coastal towns in Wales, with England itself through Chester and Bristol, and with the king's possessions in Ireland and Gascony. The rights and privileges prescribed in the charter were intended to attract to a distant and lately hostile land settlers who, by following these callings, would aid the working out of government policy and the gradual pacification of the country.

Any one familiar with the other great contemporary castles of North Wales – Conwy, Harlech, Beaumaris, Flint, Rhuddlan and Aberystwyth – will have noticed that their round towers give them a certain family resemblance which at Caernarvon is apparent only in the town wall. Here the castle is plainly a building apart, wearing an aspect of nobility all its own. This is chiefly derived from its spacious multiangular towers, which must already have been commissioned in 1283, the year in which their foundations were laid. Thus the castle would seem to have been marked out for a special role even before the birth, within its precinct, of the first English Prince of Wales. Late in 1285 or early in 1286 the constableship of Caernarvon was granted to the king's closest friend and adviser Sir Otto de Grandson (1238–1328), a Savoyard noble from Grandson on Lake Neuchâtel, of whom Edward said, "there was no one about him who could do his will better". To this same Otto had already been given the highest appointment of all, that of Justiciar of North Wales, a post equivalent to that of viceroy and carrying an annual fee of £1,000. Thus as soon as its building was well advanced, this particular castle was put in charge of the king's special confidant and lieutenant, who drew the constable's salary of £100 and retained at least nominal custody for the next four years. We cannot tell how early the decision was taken that the king would eventually confer the principality on one of his sons. It may have been intended as a matter of policy from the beginning, in which case the young Prince Alfonso would have been destined to fill the part, until his death in August 1284 laid the way open for the brother who providence and the king had decreed should be born at Caernarvon less than four months earlier. Certainly it looks very much as if, at the time the design for the castle was being prepared in 1283, it was already in view as the future official residence of the king's representative in the principality, who, if all went well, would be a prince of Edward's house. Such a purpose would demand a building of specially imposing character – a building which, though fortified with all and more than all the strength of the other castles, might yet have the appearance and provide the accommodation of a palace. It is interesting to note that James of St George, the director of the royal building works in Wales, had, a dozen years earlier, built for Edward I's cousin and friend Count Philip of Savoy a palace at St Georges-d'Espéranche, south-east of Lyon, which, though conceived on a much smaller scale, was similarly distinguished by the then relatively rare use of multiangular instead of round towers. Elsewhere in Wales they occur only at Denbigh, a castle built on the grand scale for another close associate of the king, Henry de Lacy, Earl of Lincoln, who through his mother was also related to the house of Savoy.

The name of the Eagle Tower

Of all the towers in the castle, only the Eagle Tower has kept continuously the name by which it was known at least as early as 1317. The name therefore requires explanation. Amongst the sculptured heads and other figures which at one time decorated the cresting of the

castle battlements, there are said to have been on the Eagle Tower
three eagles, one on each turret, and the tower is indeed referred to
more than once in early documents as the "Tower of the Eagles". It so
happens that an account has survived showing that one of them was
put in position in 1317 (see page 15). An eagle on the western turret
is still fairly complete, and there are the remains of a possible one on
the eastern turret; if there was one on the northern turret also, it has
perished. Had these eagles particular significance? The fact that an eagle
surmounted the Prince of Wales's shield of arms in the earliest Caernarvon borough seal,[1] and that later a seal was adopted having a shield
bearing three eagles, suggests that they had. The eagles on the tower,
like those on the seals, were almost certainly derived from the arms of
William de Grandson (d. 1335), younger brother of Otto the justiciar
and ancestor of the English branch of the Grandison family. Where
Otto's arms were charged with three *coquilles* or scallop shells, William's
were differenced with three eagles, and he and his descendants used an
eagle as their crest. He may have chosen it because it was an emblem
then much in vogue in the house of Savoy, and was the device used on
the private seal of his overlord, Count Philip. William, who was a
knight in the service of the king's brother, Edmund of Lancaster, was
one of Otto's deputies as justiciar. Eagles, moreover, were the tradi-
tional symbol of imperial power, the portrayal and embodiment of
which, at the place that was at once the seat of age-old native traditions
of Roman splendour and the chosen capital of the new English administration, was a guiding motive in the conception and design of the
castle.[2] Although not erected in their present position till 1317, the embellishments of the Eagle Tower were probably provided for from the
beginning.

Architect and builders

It can be said with reasonable certainty that the architect of Caernarvon Castle was James of St George (*c.* 1235–1308), a highly paid
master mason and military engineer whose services as master of the
king's works in Wales Edward I secured by arrangement with Count
Philip of Savoy before March 1278. Prior to that, James had been

---

[1]See the reproduction on the cover.

[2]For the evidence for the imperial aspect of Caernarvon, *see The History of the King's Works*, 1963, i, pp. 370–1.

employed successively by Peter and Philip of Savoy as their chief household architect, in which capacity he had had at least sixteen years' experience directing castle and other works in all parts of their Alpine dominion, from the Rhône east to Turin and from the Lake of Neuchâtel south to beyond the Mont Cenis. He took his surname from Philip's palace of St Georges, already referred to, which had been built under his direction between 1268 and 1274, and it was at St Georges that he probably resided until his transfer to Edward I's service in or about 1277. It is impossible to be certain about the full extent of his influence in Wales, nor can we easily draw a line between his own contribution and that of his subordinates to the design of particular features. Subject to that reservation, he controlled, besides Caernarvon, the building of Conwy, Harlech and Beaumaris, and probably of Flint, Rhuddlan, Aberystwyth and Builth as well; he directed works at Hope in 1282 and later at Criccieth, Bere and Dolwyddelan; he may also have had at least supervisory responsibility for the castles of Denbigh, Ruthin, Holt, Hawarden and Chirk.

At one time it was generally thought that Caernarvon was designed by Walter of Hereford, an English architect who was employed at Winchcombe Abbey, Gloucestershire, began the king's newly founded abbey of Vale Royal in Cheshire (1277 to 1290 or later), and was working at Amesbury, Wiltshire, in 1294–95 and at Greyfriars, London, in 1306. But there is no evidence for his being in any way concerned with Caernarvon before June 1295, by which time two thirds of the outer façade were well advanced, and the general lines, if not the details, of what remained to be done were already determined. From then onwards, apart from his absences in Scotland and London, he continued to direct the Caernarvon works until his death early in 1309. He was succeeded by his deputy, Henry of Ellerton, who remained in charge till 1323.

The probability that James of St George's staff included assistants brought from the continent is strengthened by the occurence in the works accounts of other North Wales castles of masons and engineers with names of continental origin. But apart from this small nucleus, the army of quarriers, stone-cutters, masons, smiths, carpenters, plumbers and labourers, who built Caernarvon and the rest, was an English army led by English masters and drawn from every shire in the kingdom.

It is difficult to assess how far such a building as Caernarvon owes its characteristic form to its architect and how far to the king and his circle. Royal works were under the surveillance of knights of the various households; besides William de Grandson, already mentioned, two other Savoyard kinsmen of Otto de Grandson, viz. Sir John de Bonvillars (d. 1287) and Sir Peter de Champvent, the king's chamberlain, were in positions of influence and are named in connection with the building of the castles. Much of the work was done under agreements or contracts, some at least of which are known to have been entered into with one or other of these officers, but unfortunately no original building contract for work on the North Wales castles appears to have survived.

Description

Siting and Plan

THE topography of Caernarvon as it was prior to the Industrial Revolution is obscured by the fact that one of its principal features, the little River Cadnant, is now covered from view. This makes it difficult to realise how near are the walled town and castle to occupying an island site, their bastions curving to the banks of Cadnant, Menai and Seiont, and only the relatively narrow isthmus of Castle Square joining them directly to the "mainland" (see plan inside back cover). Boydell's view (page 4), in which the course of the Cadnant lies in the dip between the Town Wall and the houses in the foreground, helps us to appreciate this. Edward I's town, built in an age when water was the best of all defences and ships the only sure link with England, was thus superbly sited. To the south the rocky shore below the castle was washed by the Seiont, there being no quay on this side until the nineteenth century; on the west the Menai flowed alongside the medieval quay; while to the north and east the Cadnant, too small to be navigable, made a natural barrier and afforded water power for the town mill. Across this barrier a long bridge, whose six stone arches, concealed by the basements of modern buildings, still carry the traffic of Eastgate Street from Turf Square to High Street, provided the main landward approach to the town. The street plan of the medieval town was simple and practical. From the East Gate (Porth Mawr) the line of the bridge approach was continued straight through to the West Gate (Porth yr Aur), where there was access to the water. Crossing this line at right-angles were the three residential streets (their northern portions now known as Northgate, Market and Church Streets), running from the Town Wall at one end to the castle ditch at the other.

Speed's map (1610) shows that there were considerable groups of houses outside the walls, along the ways leading to Bangor and Llanbeblig and on the steep hill to the east of Turf Square; here was the Welsh township, existing before and continuing side by side with the walled English borough. Bridge Street, that part of the main through road which links Turf and Castle Squares, follows, as Eastgate Street does, the line of a multi-arched bridge over the Cadnant; immediately to the east of it, where are now Pool Hill and Pool Side, was the King's Pool, a partly artificial basin in which an elaborate swan's nest was built in 1304–5 and from which a head of water ran to turn the mill,

27

Above. Plan of the castle

Below. Caernarvon from the air

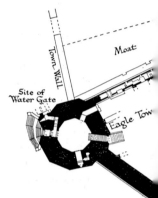

DATES OF BUILT
MAINLY 1283—9
of Eagle Tower ad
MAINLY 1296—13

Moat

Town Wall

Site of
Water Gate

Eagle Tow

CAERNARVON CASTLE

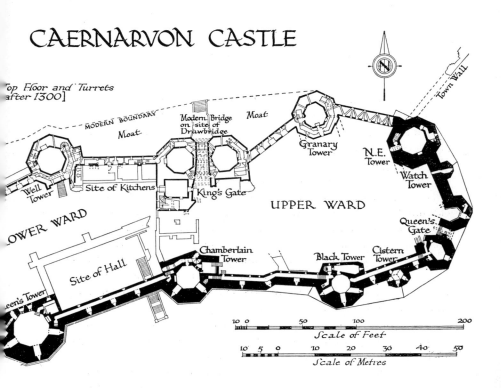

[Top Floor and Turrets
after 1300]

MODERN BOUNDARY

Moat

Moat

Modern Bridge
on site of
Drawbridge

Moat

Well
Tower

Site of Kitchens

King's Gate

Granary
Tower

N.E.
Tower

Watch
Tower

LOWER WARD

UPPER WARD

Queen's
Gate

Site of Hall

Chamberlain
Tower

Black Tower

Cistern
Tower

Queen's Tower

Town Wall

Scale of Feet

10 0   50   100   200

Scale of Metres

10 5 0   10   20   30   40   50

situated at the bottom of Mill Lane where the railway once ran behind the houses of Bridge Street.

The Castle

The visitor who has the time will do well to look first at the outside of the castle from across the Seiont, since from the farther bank of the river it is possible to comprehend at a glance the great size and massive beauty of the building. The towers, seen in order from the left (page 7), are: the Eagle Tower, the Queen's Tower, the Chamberlain Tower, the Black Tower, the Cistern Tower, and the Queen's Gate.[1] Between the Chamberlain and the Black Towers a change in the alignment of the curtain wall marks the position of the ditch which, before the present castle was built, circled the base of the Norman *motte*. Indications of the presence of the *motte* itself appear in the sloping apron or revetment of stone which begins to rise at this point and continues past the Queen's Gate to the North-east Tower. The different angles at which the walls run were governed partly by the existence of this earlier fortification and partly by the need to provide covering and cross-fire over every part of the ground below the castle. There is nevertheless symmetry in their diversity, while their level bands of vari-coloured stone give a sense of unity and cohesion to the whole composition.

Approaching more closely, the visitor will notice on the left of the Eagle Tower a stump of projecting wall on which the bands of darker stone are continued. In its thickness can be seen a portcullis groove and two blocked doorways leading from within the tower. Near the ground are the springers and jambs of a great arch, the base of which lies 4ft 6in below the road and slightly below the high water mark of ordinary tides. The remains form part of an intended Water Gate across the western end of the castle ditch, through which, had it ever been completed, water-borne supplies could have been carried at high tides to the door in the basement of the Well Tower (page 33).

The visitor should now leave the waterfront and turn through the opening in the Town Wall, passing along the north front of the castle to the main entrance. A point of particular interest immediately beyond the Eagle Tower is the change of build between work executed before (to the west) and after (to the east) 1295. Evidence of this can be seen

---

[1]Except for the Eagle Tower, all the towers have been known by different names at different times. The Well Tower was so called in 1343, but the other names are unhistorical.

in a break in the coursing of the masonry and in the termination of the bands of darker stone. There is a similar break near the western angle of the North-east Tower. When the moat was reopened in the nineteenth century it was not possible to restore its full original width. much of which, particularly at the eastern end, is now covered by the street known as Castle Ditch.

King's Gate. No building in Britain exhibits more strikingly the immense strength of medieval fortification than the great entrance gateway of Caernarvon Castle. To gain access to the outer or lower ward it would have been necessary to cross a drawbridge (the present fixed bridge and steps are modern) and pass through five doors and under six portcullises, with a right-angled turn as one passed from the main gate passage to the smaller passage (probably never completed) along the south side of the gatehouse, at the end of which there was to be a second drawbridge. The observant visitor will be able to detect traces of all these obstacles, the bearings for the drawbridges, the draw-bar holes and rebates for the doors (some opening inwards, others outwards), and the grooves for the portcullises. At each successive division arrow loops and spy-holes flank and command the approach from different levels, while in the vaulting above there are groups of "murder holes" (no less than nine of them survive) to threaten assailants and allow water to be poured down to extinguish any fire that might be started against the gates. Beyond the line of the third portcullis, doors on either side lead to the porters' rooms which occupied the ground floors of the adjacent octagonal towers, and which now house temporary buildings used in connection with the administration and maintenance of the castle.

To reach the upper part of the gatehouse the visitor should turn to the right at the end of the gate passage; a door on the right opens to a stair in the rearward part of the building. This leads up to a wall passage at first-floor level, from which there is a modern footbridge across the north-west gate tower to the room above the main gate passage. Like the corresponding room in the gatehouse at Harlech Castle, this was a chapel, though its position prevented normal orientation. The principal window is on the north; its main lights were shuttered, only the quatrefoil head being grooved for glass. There is a trefoiled piscina. It will be remarked that, when raised, two of the portcullises came up through the chapel floor, an arrangement which emphasises the fact

Eagle Tower

that in a medieval castle the great gate was seldom opened, and then only for the briefest interval. The wall passages at this level contain arrow slits grouped in such a way that, although only six openings are apparent from without, double that number of archers could discharge their shafts through them simultaneously.

Above the chapel and the tower rooms on either side of it there was to have been a large hall, 60ft long. The principal features of its north wall, apparently the only part to be completed, can be seen from the floor below: there are three large two-light transomed windows with window-seats and quatrefoiled heads, and, over the gate, two more groups of three-in-one arrow slits. The surviving roof corbels have finely decorated heads.

Kitchens. Against the curtain wall between the King's Gate and the Well Tower (the next tower to the west) were the castle kitchens. The springer of a great arch, and bonding for a cross partition, both built contemporaneously with the curtain, show that it was intended to build the whole in stone, but the slight foundation walls on the courtyard side suggest that, as built, the kitchens were largely half-timbered structures. On the north side there is a trough for the water supply, piped through the thickness of the wall from a tank in the Well Tower. At the west end are remains of seatings for two coppers, with fireplaces below them; it has been suggested that the wall cavity behind them was used for smoking meat.

Well Tower. There are two entrances to the Well Tower from the courtyard, one at ground, the other at basement level. The visitor should first descend the steps to the latter, noting on the way down the position of a door which originally barred the entry. It is possible in the Well Tower to obtain a particularly good "cross-section" view of what was involved in the construction of each and all of the ten major towers of the castle, for here none of the timber floors of the upper storeys have been restored and the tower is open from the basement to the sky, allowing the characteristic details of each room to be seen at a glance from below. Including the basement there were in all four storeys, and this was so in the majority of the northern towers. At basement level there is on the north-west a wide gateway, originally defended with outer and inner doors, portcullis and "murder holes", designed to allow water-borne supplies for the adjacent kitchens and service rooms to be brought in from the moat (cf. page 30), At each of the three upper levels there is a pair of square holes on opposite sides of the tower, which, with supporting corbels below, carried the great cross-beams on which were laid the joists of the main floors. Each of these upper rooms has its own fireplace and its privy reached by a passage in the thickness of the outside wall, arrangements which are common to practically all the rooms in the castle. The ground-floor fireplace provides a good example of typical lintel construction, with its three rows of joggled or interlocking keystones, while the fireplace on the first floor, which contained the principal room, has a fine projecting hood; both types will be found in other parts of the castle. The tower was left unfinished in the fourteenth century and much of its top, including the whole of the surmounting turret, is modern work dating from the time of Sir Llewelyn Turner.

The well which gives the tower its name is contained in a rectangular annexe attached to the east side; it extends nearly 50ft below courtyard level. The well chamber is on the ground floor and is reached by a passage from the entrance door near the top of the basement steps; in it should be noted the stone seating for a lead-lined cistern, which could be kept filled from the buckets raised from the well, and from which inclined pipes run in different directions through the thickness of the wall to supply the nearby kitchens. The well shaft extends upwards, allowing the water to be drawn at first-floor level also.

From near the well chamber a winding stair leads to the upper "floors" and to the turret; on the landings there are openings from which some of the structural features seen from below can be studied at closer range. From the second-floor vestibule, steps lead up eastwards to the wall-walk, which can be followed at this level across the upper part of the King's Gate, through the Granary and North-east Towers (in both of which there are stairs down to ground level), past the Watch Tower and so on as far as the Queen's Gate. Westwards there is a wall-walk at first-floor level to the Eagle Tower; on the second floor there is a doorway with a modern barrier across it – this was similarly intended to lead on to an upper wall-walk, but the curtain wall at this point was never carried above first-floor level. Visitors who are following this handbook should descend the stairs again and, on emerging into the courtyard, turn right towards the Eagle Tower. Against the curtain wall linking the two towers are the fireplace (restored), roof corbels and partition bonding stones of a range of rooms, possibly never completed or perhaps built with timber-framed inner walls.

Eagle Tower. This is the greatest of all the castle's towers and was probably at first intended to provide accommodation for Sir Otto de Grandson, the king's lieutenant and first Justiciar of North Wales. Everything about it (except perhaps, by modern standards, the internal lighting) is designed on a magnificent scale. Like the other northern towers it comprises a basement and three storeys, but there is more generous provision of wall-chambers and its group of three lofty turrets is a feature believed to be unique. The basement forms as it were an ante-chamber through which anyone coming to Caernarvon by water would gain direct entrance to the castle. The more normal approach, however, is from the opposite direction by steps leading down from the courtyard. From the door at the bottom of these steps a further flight leads down through the thickness of the wall into the basement itself, which, like the three great rooms above, is ten-sided and measures some 30 to 35ft across. On the side facing the steps is the passage leading in, through a portcullis and strongly barred double doors, from the waterside. From this passage there are stairs communicating with the intended Water Gate (cf. page 30), while another passage would have led to the basement of the buildings against the north curtain wall. When all the doors are closed the room receives its only natural light from a tall arrow slit in the south wall; the embrasure, in one side of which there is a passage leading to a privy, conveys a good impression of the wall's immense thickness, here about 18ft.

The ground-floor room is approached through a vestibule from the courtyard. Though dark, it is of noble proportions, and there is a large hooded fireplace. The laid-up colours of the Royal Welch Fusiliers are displayed on the walls. The floor and ceiling, the latter a close replica of the original arrangement, date from 1911–14,[1] as do those above and in a number of the other towers. Doors lead from the main room to various passages and octagonal and hexagonal chambers contrived in the thickness of the walls, some of the latter notable for the fine workmanship of their vaults: the little chamber opposite the entrance contained the gear for raising the portcullis of the postern below, while the passage in the north wall would have led to a room serving the same purpose over the adjacent Water Gate and provided direct communication between the castle and the Court Hall to the

---

[1]All the beams and joists inserted at this time are of Quebec oak; the two beams on the first floor of the Eagle Tower have a span of 40ft 3in.

north (cf. page 48). An octagonal chamber on the south-east side, reached from the foot of the stair to the upper floors, was probably a chapel; it is lighted from the east, and a small rectangular aperture (now closed) in the inner wall would have enabled an occupant of the main room to observe the celebrant. The same arrangement will be noted in similarly placed rooms in the Queen's and Chamberlain Towers.

The first-floor room is similar, but better lighted. It now houses an exhibition of late-medieval armour, but it was originally the principal apartment of the tower. There is the same elaborate provision of subsidiary accommodation in the thickness of the walls, with the south-east angle occupied, as on the floor below, by an octagonal chapel; here the purpose is made certain by the remains of a trefoiled piscina, and there is a corresponding rectangular opening through to the main room. Special interest has been attached in the past to a small rectangular room on the north side as being the alleged birthplace of the first English Prince of Wales, and since the nineteenth century plausibility has been lent to the identification by the insertion in the window of the arms of Albert Edward, Prince of Wales (afterwards King Edward VII). But, as has been shown earlier (page 10), it is most unlikely that the Eagle Tower had been built to this height by the time of Edward of Caernarvon's birth in April 1284. One feels, too, that were it not for the fact that a century ago the *main* rooms of the tower were without floors and roofs, such a momentous event would hardly have been associated with so mean a location.

Evidence has been found that, for some time at least, the tower did not at first extend above the first floor, the second floor and the three surmounting watch towers being additions completed in the second decade of the fourteenth century. An indication of this is the up-and-down slope of the offset where the first-floor ceiling rests on the walls, showing that they were at first built to take a low-pitched outer roof at this point.

The topmost room, entered directly from the stair, is well lit by a pair of two-light windows set in tall pointed-arch embrasures with stepped window-seats. The fireplace has a flush lintel with interlocking keystones. There are rectangular wall chambers on the north and north-east, the latter perhaps a kitchen, while a passage on the south leads to a privy.

The main stair leads on to the roof of the tower, whence it is continued in one of three hexagonal turrets; in the most westerly of these there is a stair which is accessible to visitors. The battlements, both on the tower and on the turrets, are unrestored, and their copings preserve the remains of the numerous stone figures with which they were originally decorated; some were evidently helmeted heads, while on the west turret an eagle, much weathered, is still easily recognisable (cf. page 24). Remains of similar embellishments will be noticed in other parts of the castle.

Queen's Tower. The Queen's Tower is linked to the Eagle Tower by a length of curtain with wall-walks at two levels, the lower of which was evidently intended to be completed as a covered passage like those further to the east. The two towers have common internal dimensions and wall thicknesses, but here there are only three storeys, the ground floor corresponding in a sense to the basement floor of the Eagle Tower, which likewise had only the three storeys to begin with. At the north-west corner there is a newel stair from the courtyard to the leads, communicating with the two upper rooms and their encircling wall passages. These latter are continuous round the outer sides of the tower, taking the place of the separate polygonal wall-chambers provided in the Eagle Tower. Each floor is also equipped with a subsidiary room at the north-east corner, of which the topmost was certainly and each of the others probably a chapel. The main rooms are lighter than those of the Eagle Tower, being provided with good windows on the inward or courtyard side, in addition to obtaining borrowed light through the wall passages. The roof turret is rather larger than the others in the castle, and at half height has a small hexagonal chamber from which a narrow flight of steps continues to the summit. A lintel above these steps contains a round hole for holding the base of a flag-staff, an interesting corroboration of the name "Tour de la Banere", or Banner Tower, borne by this tower in the fourteenth century.

The Queen's Tower now houses the regimental museum of the Royal Welch Fusiliers, to serve which a modern staircase has been erected in the space formerly occupied by the subsidiary rooms.

Chamberlain Tower. To reach the Chamberlain Tower the visitor may descend again to the courtyard and walk along to the principal entrance, which is by a door at the bottom of the tower's stair turret immediately opposite the King's Gate; or it may be approached along either of the two wall passages which run, one above the other

for the full length of the intervening curtain. This curtain formed the south wall of the 100ft long Great Hall; of the end walls of the Hall, only the parts formed by the Queen's and Chamberlain Towers still stand, but there is a fine moulded plinth on the remaining footings at the west end. Within the site of the east end of the Hall, where were probably the buttery and pantry, there are steps leading down to a postern opening towards the Seiont.

The Chamberlain Tower (called also the Treasury Tower and the Record Tower) is smaller than those previously described, and contains three 22ft wide octagonal rooms; annexed to each one, on the north-east, is a rectangular chamber, that on the first floor being a chapel. In the corresponding chamber above, the floor has not been restored, nor is there any means of access to it, there being no communication with the principal room. Continuous wall passages circle the outer sides of the tower at first- and second-floor levels. On the ground floor a door at the north-west corner formerly led directly into the Great Hall. The stair is in the centre of the north side and is accessible to the top of the turret. The battlements and cresting of the tower proper are original, those of the turret restored. The only surviving stone chimney in the castle may be noted on the leads at the back of the turret.

Between the Chamberlain Tower and the Black Tower the wall passages are continued in the curtain. That on the first floor is now unroofed, but was certainly intended to form a covered gallery like the one below; there is also an open wall-walk at battlement level. The change in direction which the curtain makes mid-way between the towers arises from the fact that at this point it crosses the site of the ditch of the earlier *motte* (cf. page 30).

Black Tower. The Black Tower contains two small ten-sided rooms instead of the usual three or four. This is partly because, although it looks much the same height as the other towers to the west of it, it is in reality built against the side of the former *motte*, so that much of what appears as tower externally is in fact a great solid five-sided bastion buttressing the made ground of the Norman earthwork; the same is true of the lowest stage of the towers of the Queen's Gate. Entrance to the Black Tower is from the wall passages on either side of it, there being no door communicating directly with the courtyard. A stair in the north-west corner gives access to the first-floor rooms, the leads and the surmounting turret. The upper storey has a chapel on the north or courtyard side, the floor of which has not been destroyed, and there is a small ante-chapel to the west of it; at courtyard level the corresponding space is occupied by a single room with windows on the north and east, the use of which is unknown. At the top of the tower short flights of steps serve to continue the wall-walk across the leads from one side of the tower to the other. This arrangement is not found elsewhere in the castle, and it is possible that it was intended to add a third storey and bring the height of the Black Tower up to that of the adjacent Queen's Gate; these upper flights of stairs would then have been replaced by a level wall-passage similar to that on the floor below.

Cistern Tower. The arrangement of the passages and wall-walk in the curtain east of the Black Tower repeats that on the west. From the lower passage a door opens directly into the lower part of the Cistern

Tower, which at this level contains a small hexagonal chamber with three embrasures and arrow loops towards the south; its finely worked groined vault recalls those in the lower wall-chambers of the Eagle Tower. Above the vault is the open stone-lined rainwater tank from which the tower takes its name; it can be seen from the wall-walk, which may be reached by one of the narrow stairs leading up from the embrasures of the middle (unroofed) passage of the curtain. A stone outlet channel which runs through the thickness of the wall and discharges through a shaft in the Queen's Gate will be noticed crossing one of the nearby arrow slits. The top of the tower has an unfinished appearance, and was no doubt intended to be carried up to match the level of the top of the Queen's Gate.

Queen's Gate. Seen from without, the east gate of the castle is a monument of great majesty, dignified in conception, simple of line, imposing yet unostentatious. Seen from within, it conveys all the interest that attaches to a building seen in cross-section through having been left half finished more than six centuries ago. The outward façade owes its unusual character to the elevated level of the gate passage and the resulting great height of the containing arch in which the gate itself is framed. The level of the gate passage was, of course, dictated by the presence of the Norman *motte*, on or against which all this eastern part of the castle is built. The decorative banding of darker-coloured stone also makes a particularly effective contribution. The battlements are modern restorations, and it is fair to assume that the originals would have been decked with heads and finials like those of which we have noted traces elsewhere.

On plan the gatehouse consists of a central passage and drawbridge pit flanked by two unfinished polygonal towers which project as half-octagons from the line of the converging north and south curtains. To the rear of the gate passage, and slightly to the south of it, an inner gate and portcullis was planned; the lower courses of one side of this gate were built and will be seen projecting inwards at the end of the south curtain wall. The wall passage, here unvaulted, which we have traced at slightly varying levels all the way from the other side of the Queen's Tower, was to be continued round the twin towers of the Queen's Gate and thence carried along the north side of the castle; where the backs of those towers are left unfinished the wall passage is seen in section in two openings across which are modern oak barriers.

At courtyard level each tower contained an irregular-shaped porter's room one on either side of the gate passage, the northern of which still remains open to the courtyard. At the upper level there was to be a hall extending over the full area of the gatehouse; no doubt the light it would have obtained from the three arrow loops on the east was intended to be supplemented by the provision of larger windows in the unbuilt western side.

The lofty position of the Queen's Gate makes it naturally less vulnerable than its counterpart towards the old town, and its defensive equipment is proportionately less elaborate. It was, however, to be well provided with "murder holes": five are visible, two of them showing in section towards the courtyard. Much evidence remains for the working of the drawbridge (or, more correctly, "turning" bridge), and may be examined from the railed platform which has been constructed in the outer part of the gate passage. On either side can be seen the bearings for the roller on which the bridge pivoted; below the platform is the deep pit which took the counterpoise weight of the bridge when the latter was in the raised position, its back wall built as a revetment to the earlier *motte* behind it. When the bridge was lowered, its outer end was designed to rest on the tip of a stone-built ramp approached up gently graded steps (like those, for example, in the barbican at Denbigh or from the Water Gate at Harlech) and so placed as to leave a narrow chasm between it and the castle. A similar ascent to the drawbridge at Conwy Castle survived until the beginning of the present century, but it is not known if the Caernarvon work was ever completed.

The fact that the medieval builders completed the outer façade of the Queen's Gate while leaving the accommodation at the back of it to be finished later is interesting evidence of the importance attached to erecting the full circuit of a castle's (or a castle and town's) main defensive walls as early as possible, so as to afford protection behind which internal development could be left to proceed by more leisurly stages. The same thing has already been noted in regard to the King's Gate, and the identical practice was also followed in the building of Beaumaris Castle at the other end of the Menai Strait. Much of the building work which went gradually on at Caernarvon between 1295 and 1330 consisted in building up the inward complements of structures whose outer façades were the only parts to be completed in the 1280s.

Watch Tower. The short section of curtain wall separating the Queen's Gate from the North-east Tower is pierced at intermediate level by what is in effect a continuation of one of the southern wall passages, the continuity being broken only by the unbuilt back walls of the gatehouse. From the wall-walk above (which for the same reason can only be approached by way of the North-east Tower) a door leads to the upper part of a slender turret now generally known as the Watch Tower. The top was a look-out point, and had a pentise roof to give cover to the watchman. The battlements both here and on the nearby wall-walk retain traces of the grooves in which were hung wooden shutters for protecting the archers. The basement of the turret (not accessible to visitors) is entered at courtyard level through a door opening to a passage cut through the thickness of the curtain.

North-east Tower. The North-east Tower is octagonal and of two storeys only. The ground-floor room houses the Investiture exhibition. The roof of the upper floor has not been replaced, so that this room is now open to the sky; its hooded fireplace is for the most part a restoration, but parts of the jambs are original. The stair is at the north-west corner; the surmounting turret has an unusual feature in that the arrow loops, instead of being set in the merlons, are placed between them. The characteristic wall passages of the southern side of the castle are continued round the outer sides of the tower but do not go on beyond it; this is because, as the plan (on page 29) shows, the work of the earlier building period terminates here, and wall passages were not provided in the northern curtains which from this point to the Eagle Tower date (except for much of the revetments below courtyard level) from 1295 and later.

Granary Tower. One of the most interesting features in the castle is the multiple grouping of arrow slits at two levels in the curtain walls on either side of the Granary Tower, a refinement of military engineering previously encountered in describing the upper floors of the King's Gate. The fire power which such arrangements enabled to be brought to bear on a limited front must, by the standards of the time, have been devastating.

In many respects the Granary Tower duplicates the Well Tower. It is octagonal, of four storeys surmounted by a turret, and has a wall passage on the courtyard side at ground level; this leads to a vaulted well-chamber, the well of which always contains a supply of good water. The stair is at the north-east. Of the main rooms only that on the top floor, which is unroofed, can be seen by visitors; it is crossed by the wall-walk along the top of the curtains. This route may be followed across the King's Gate to the Well Tower and so down to the courtyard again.

The visitor who has traversed even half the wall passages and battlement walks of Caernarvon Castle, who has climbed a few of its stairs and viewed only one or two of its great rooms, may well depart in greater wonder than he came. Why was this great fortress built here, and why was it conceived on so vast a scale? Why were all these rooms provided, and who was to use them? The answer has been partially given already. The builders of Caernarvon at the end of the thirteenth century looked on it as the capital of a new dominion, a capital from which, nominally at all times and personally perhaps at some times, a new dynasty of princes would rule an ancient principality. Caernarvon Castle therefore had to be capable, when occasion required, of adequately accommodating the household of the king's eldest son, with his Council, his family, his guests and all who attended on them; in that is implied the capacity to store the treasure, the wardrobe, the records, the provender, the supplies of all kinds required to sustain a great medieval household in appropriate state on its journeyings and sojournings, as well as to accommodate such officials as the constable and the watchmen, together with a small garrison, whose presence in the castle was a permanency. History, in the event, seldom if ever fulfilled for the castle the high role intended for it, and in practice, in the fourteenth century at any rate, it had little more to do than serve as the depot for the armament and building maintenance of the other North Wales castles.[1]

The Town Walls

The circuit of walls and towers enclosing the medieval borough has survived unbroken, It extends from near the north-east to near the north-west corner of the castle, a distance of about 800 yards. Its eight towers and two twin-towered gateways are spaced at intervals of approximately 70 yards. In this brief description only the principal points of interest are noted. The order followed is from opposite the North-east Tower of the castle round to the Eagle Tower, the wall

[1]The two guns in the courtyard bear the cypher of Charles III of Spain (1759–88), and are trophies of the Peninsular War.

towers being numbered to correspond with the numbers on the plan at the end of the handbook.

From the Castle to the East Gate (3). The eastern part of the street known as Castle Ditch occupies the filled-in northern half of the great moat between the castle and the town, only a part of which is to be seen today. At its eastern end this moat opened into another which, as the eighteenth-century engravings show, bordered the town wall and continued past the Queen's Gate to the bank of the Seiont. The town wall proper did not cross the castle moat, but, as at Conwy, terminated on its edge, where is now the footpath of Castle Ditch and where, except for a height of about 7ft above present ground level, the masonry of the wall finishes abruptly on a clean vertical line. From this point a lower and less massive wall, the roughly broken commencement of which contrasts with the smooth face above, was carried down to the full depth of the moat and across to the castle; signs of its former junction with the foot of the North-east Tower may still be observed.

From Castle Ditch to East Gate (3) there are three sections of wall with two intervening towers. Against the inner side of the first section are the remains of one of the stairs which gave access to the wall-walk and to the upper floor of the adjacent tower (1) (other well-preserved stairs may be seen beside Towers 4 and 6). The stair has the effect of doubling the thickness of the wall, which is here pierced by a postern gate, formerly closed by a portcullis as well as by wooden doors. This was called the Green Gate, from its proximity to the Green (now Castle Square), the name being preserved in Greengate Street which here follows the line of the town ditch. The tower (1) is well preserved on the outside; though all its inner facing has been stripped, exaggerating the interior dimensions, it is possible to see a sloping line of seven holes, which show that when the tower was built an inclined scaffold was used. The next section of wall has lately been cleared of a row of nineteenth-century dwellings, last survivors of those which until the 1930s hid the wall all the way along Greengate Street and Bank Quay. Tower (2) stands to the full height of its battlements. On either side of it may be seen the fragments of the stone revetment originally built to retain the steep banks which foot the adjoining stretches of wall. The interior of this tower can be seen from an alley off Hole-in-the-Wall Street; the facework is intact, and shows signs of the building's former adaptation to house a cottage. The wall from here to the East Gate (3) has been largely refaced without and is concealed by houses within; the older masonry is less regularly coursed and is easily distinguishable from the pinkish stone of the newer.

The East Gate (3). This was the principal landward entrance to the town. Something of its original appearance is shown in the eighteenth-century engravings, where the barbican gate which formerly stood in front of it (see p. 48) can also be seen. Between the barbican and the main gate there was at first a drawbridge across the town ditch. The rooms above the gateway served from the first to accommodate the Exchequer, established by the Statute of 1284 as the administrative and financial centre for the counties of Caernarvon, Anglesey and Merioneth. An account of 1310–11 mentions the provision of a louvre, by which the exchequer chamber would be lighted from above; the successor of this louvre can be seen in the three Buck engravings of Caernarvon published in 1742. Since 1767, when the upper part of the gate was adapted as a Town Hall, the building has been used for municipal purposes; alterations made in 1833 and commemorated by a tablet in the main archway were swept away in 1873 to make way for a new Guildhall and offices. These in turn were demolished in 1963, and the remains of the twin medieval gate towers, freed for the first time for many years of structures built above and against them, can now be seen in their proper relationship to the town walls fronting Bank Quay and Greengate Street.

From the East Gate (3) *to the waterfront.* Beyond the East Gate (3) is an angle tower (4) standing to the full height of its battlements, which retain their cresting with the remains of finials. The length of wall between this and the next tower (5) is the best preserved of all, the merlons, containing the bases of arrow slits, rising well-defined above the level of the wall-walk. The opening to Northgate Street is relatively modern, as are those to Market Street and Church Street, only the last-named being shown in one of the 1742 engravings. Between towers (5) and (6) the wall has been pierced in recent times to give access to tower (5) and light to a house in Market Street; this part of the wall still shows evidence of the whitening applied to its surface at the back of the dwellings which, until the 1930s, entirely screened it from view. The early fourteenth-century chapel of St Mary (see p. 49) is built against the inside of the wall beyond tower (6); the angle tower (7) is incorporated in it and serves as its vestry. The inward faces of towers (4) and (6), together with their bridges and adjacent stairs, are well preserved and may be seen from within the wall. These bridges, originally of timber and later renewed in stone, gave continuity to the different sections of the wall-walk; their importance is illustrated by an order to the chamberlain of North Wales in 1347 "to repair the bridges on the walls of the said town . . . so that it may be possible to walk safely on the walls and defend the town in case of peril". Tower (5), which is not accessible, has an inserted brick vault in its lowest section and, like tower (1), has lost all its interior facework.

From the north-west corner (7) *to the Castle.* Allowing for the fact that the wall battlements are wanting and for those on the towers being modern replacements, the long stretch of wall facing the Menai retains its medieval atmosphere and charm in a way that is denied to the parts engulfed by the growth of the later town. Here from the beginning was the quay, and in the Bucks' time (1742) the southern part of what is now the Anglesey Hotel was the Custom House. The first quay, constructed of wood in and after 1283, was burned in the troubles of 1294–95; it was rebuilt in stone in the first quarter of the fourteenth century. The towers on the waterfront are occupied and inaccessible to visitors. Tower (8) contains a dwelling, its door, windows, battlements and castellated chimney all being of nineteenth-century date. The West Gate (9), a twin-towered gatehouse with small projecting barbican, houses the Royal Welsh Yacht Club; here also the windows, battlements and moulded strings, all of pink sandstone, are modern, as is the brick vault of the gate passage, the insertion of which has blocked the tops of the portcullis grooves. The lower part of the next tower (10) is occupied in connection with the adjacent County Offices, into which the nineteenth-century buildings of the former county gaol have been lately converted. The presence within the wall at this point of the Police Station (1853) and County Hall (1863), the latter containing the Crown Court, serves to recall the fact that the administration of justice has been carried on on this site in unbroken sequence for nearly seven centuries; here was the court-house and the justiciar's "inn" or lodging, in reference to which we read in the strange mixture of Latin, French and English of an account of 1435, of repairs to the "domus session apud le Justice court", and also of the hall of pleas and the justiciar's kitchen.

At the western end of the Castle Ditch the town wall is pierced by a relatively modern opening on the site of an older and narrower postern, remains of which, including five re-used pieces of portcullis groove, may be detected in the existing masonry. The original end of the wall is marked by a straight joint a few feet to the south; this break is in line with the edge of the moat and corresponds to the similar vertical termination of the wall, referred to earlier, at the opposite end of Castle Ditch. The continuation of the wall at full height directly across to the castle was not part of the original plan and dates from an alteration authorised in 1326. The intention of the thirteenth-century builders was to erect against this side of the Eagle Tower a massive Water Gate, part of which, begun contemporaneously with the tower itself and indicating something similar in scale and conception to St Thomas's Gate at the Tower of London, may still be seen. This would have allowed passage at high water for a shallow-draft barge or lighter to enter the moat and unload its cargo through the door in the basement of the Well Tower. It is clear that the scheme was never completed as planned. As late as 1435 much work was done on a "new gate called le Watergate", *alias* "the outer postern on the quay beside the Eagle Tower" ("pro posterne exteriori del key juxta le Egle toure"); the reference is probably to the building of the above-mentioned postern leading from the quay into the town.

The Town Bridge. Eastgate Street, running from Turf Square to the East Gate (3), is carried on a medieval bridge of six arches, one of which (that over the junction of Greengate Street and Bank Quay – see page 45) is still open to view; remains of the others have been exposed from time to time in the course of excavations for new buildings on either side of the street. The purpose of the bridge was to carry the approach to the walled town across the low-lying Cadnant; the stream now runs underground through an arch whose upstream face is visible from basement premises below No. 12 Eastgate Street. As built in the 1280s the bridge was a wooden structure; this was destroyed by the rebels in 1294–95, and its rebuilding in stone was put in hand in 1301 or 1302. In front of the main gate of the town the bridge was spanned by a smaller battlemented gateway, repairs to which are mentioned in an account of 1310. Here the tolls on merchandise were collected, and in 1310–11 a building was erected outside the gate to serve as a "Tolbothe".

The Chapel of St Mary. Until the beginning of the fourteenth century Llanbeblig church sufficed for the needs of the new English borough as well as of the older Welsh *maenor*. In 1303 Edward, Prince of Wales, licensed Henry of Ellerton, a burgess of Caernarvon and deputy master of the works, "to build a chantry chapel in the town of Carnarvan on his burgage there . . . and to assign to the chapel the said burgage and 30 acres of land in Carnarvan . . . . for the sustenance of a chaplain". Thus was founded, within the walls of Caernarvon, the chapel of St Mary, which has remained throughout its history a chapel of ease to the mother church situated at Llanbeblig without the walls of Segontium. Ellerton's property lay in the town's north-west angle, and it was therefore possible for him to incorporate the town wall in his new building. A reference to glazing the windows of the chapel in 1316 (by which time Ellerton had succeeded Walter of Hereford as chief master mason at Caernarvon) may probably be taken as indicating its completion at about that date. The building has been much restored, but the arcades are original fourteenth-century features; the carved heads of a man and woman in one of the spandrels may well be portraits of Henry of Ellerton and his wife.

Fully documented accounts of the castle and town walls will be found in the *Caernarvonshire Survey and Inventory* of the Royal Commission on Ancient Monuments, vol. ii (1960), pp. 124–50, and *The History of the King's Works*, vol. i (1963), pp. 369–95.

Castell Caernarfon

HANES Y CASTELL

Dechreuwyd adeiladu Castell Caernarfon ym 1283 ar safle Norman-aidd a berthynai i'r cyfnod c. 1090, ac nid oeddent wedi gorffen ei adeiladu pan roisant y gorau i weithio arno tua 1330 Fe'i cynlluniwyd gan Edward I i gadarnhau ei fuddugoliaeth tros Llywelyn Tywysog Cymru a Dafydd ei frawd ac i wasanaethu fel canolfan seremoniol llinach frenhinol Lloegr a fyddai'n llywodraethu Eryri o hyn allan.

O'r cychwyn cyntaf fe'i bwriadwyd i fod yn symbol yn ogystal ag adeilad milwrol. Yn ôl traddodiad llafar a ymgorfforwyd yn rhamant Macsen Wledig, fe geir dolen sy'n cysylltu Caernarfon a Rhufain. Yn y chwedl honno sonnir am Ymerawdwr o'r gorffennol pell yn ymweld â gwlad fynyddig, ac yno ar aber rhyw afon fe welodd ddinas gaerog a chastell mawreddog a'i dyrau o bob lliw. Yn fwriadol y creodd Edward dref a chastell fel y rhain a charient rai o nodweddion arbennig dinas Ymerodrol Caergystennin–y tyrau amlochrog yn frenhinol a chylch o gerrig lliw o'u cwmpas. Yr oedd hyd yn oed 'Borth Aur' yn y dref newydd, a Phorth yr Aur y gelwir ef hyd heddiw gan Gymry Cymraeg Caernarfon.

Er i'r Brenin ei gynllunio'n balas tywysog ni fu'r un tywysog yn byw yno erioed. Yng Nghaernarfon yn siŵr iawn y ganwyd y Tywsog Edward, a hynny fwy na thebyg mewn llerty pren ar safle'r adeiladau oedd yn dechrau cael eu codi y pryd hwnnw. Chwe chan mlynedd yn ddiweddarach y defnyddiwyd y castell fel ei bwriadwyd pan gynhaliwyd seremoni arwisgo Tywysog Edward arall yn Nghaer-narfon ym 1911. Yn hanesyddol rhaid mai yn Rhuddlan y cwrddodd y Brenin â'r Cymry ac addo iddynt "dywysog a anwyd yng Nghymru, na fedrai air o Saesneg ac na allai undyn bardduo ei fuchedd na'i sgwrs." Cyfeirio yr oedd wrth gwrs at y baban, y Tywysog Edward o Gaernarfon.

ADEILADAU A NODWEDDION ARBENNIG

Porth y Brenin—y brif fynedfa i'r castell, ac uwch ei phen y mae cofgolofn Edward II a godwyd ym 1320 a'r blynyddoedd yn gadael eu hôl yn drwm iawn arni. Mae nodweddion manwl ac amddiffynnol rhodfa'r porth yn eithaf clir. Dyma bwll y bont, ac ar hwn y troai colyn y bont, dyma rigolau'r pyrthcwlis, pyst y pyrth a'r 'tyllau llofruddio' uwchben. Ni orffennwyd cefn tŷ'r porth.

Tŵr yr Eryr—Hwn yw'r tŵr mwyaf yn y castell. Y mae ynddo bedwar llawr heb gyfri'r un o dan y ddaear. Ar ben un twred y mae eryr carreg. Yn y cyfrifon adeiladu am 1316–1317 ceir sôn manwl am osod yr eryr yn ei le. Yn ôl traddodiad yma y ganwyd y Tywysog Edward o Gaernarfon, stori sy'n mynd nôl mor bell â 1724 beth bynnag, ond yn ôl y cofnod hanesyddol mae'n annhebyg i'r tywysog gael ei eni yn y tŵr a saif yma heddiw.

Porth y Frenhines—Fe saif 40 troedfedd yn uwch nag arwynebedd y tir y tu allan oherwydd fe ymgorfforir yn y pen hwn o'r castell y safle Normanaidd cynnar. Os codwyd un o gwbl, ar hyd ramp hir mae'n siŵr y rhedai'r ffordd at y fynedfa. Ni orffennwyd adeiladu cefn tŷ'r porth, ond yr oedd yna borth allanol a phont dro fel yr un ym Mhorth y Brenin. Ar y balconi a godir yn arbennig ar amgylchiad brenhinol y saif Brenin neu'r Tywysog fel y gall y Cymry sydd wedi ymgynnull ar Sgŵar y Castell ei weld.

Tŵr y Gwyliwr—Gellir cyrraedd brig y tŵr hwn, y teneuaf yn y castell, o lwybr y mur. Ar yr amddiffynfeydd gerllaw, fe welir y rhigolau lle troai'r cloriau pren i amddiffyn y saethyddion. Yma efallai y safai'r gŵr hwnnw a'i utgorn, y sonnir amdano yng nghyfrifon y gwaith am 1319 a 1320 i seinio'n ddyddiol yr amserau i ddechrau a gorffen gweithio.

Tyredau, amddiffynfeydd, rhodfeydd yn y muriau ac agennau'r saethyddion. Y mae deg twred yn y castell, ac y mae'r rhan fwyaf ohonynt a'r llwybrau amddiffynnol ar hyd y muriau a'r rhodfeydd yn y muriau yn agored i'r cyhoedd. Oherwydd y llwybrau a'r rhodfeydd, fe allai'r milwyr symud yn gyflym o un tŵr ac o un agen saethu i'r llall ac anelu i unrhyw gyfeiriad ar unwaith. Cynlluniwyd yr agennau saethu yn y mur ar bob ochr i Dŵr y Granari fel y gallai tri gŵr saethu yr un pryd o unrhyw un ohonynt, neu un gŵr drwy unrhyw ddau ohonynt.

Ffynhonnau, dŵr, glendid. Y mae dwy ffynnon yn y castell, un i bob ward, ac yn Nhŵr y Seston a adawyd heb ei orffen, fe adeiladwyd tanc dal dŵr glaw. Mewn ystafelloedd yn y muriau y darparwyd lleoedd ymolchi etc. i'r milwyr, a châi'r carthion eu cario oddi yno trwy gwteri serth yn y muriau i ffos y castell neu i'r afon.

Glossary

BAILEY	Courtyard or ward.
CORBEL	A projection from a wall, intended to support a weight.
CRENELLATION	Opening in the upper part of a parapet; a sign of fortification, e.g., a licence to crenellate was the equivalent of a permit to fortify a residence.
CURTAIN	The wall enclosing a courtyard.
DRAWBRIDGE	A wooden bridge, which can be raised towards a gateway by means of chains or ropes attached to its outer end.
EMBRASURE	Recess in the thickness of a wall, providing space for window-seats or elbow-room for arrow slits.
GARDEROBE	Latrine.
HALL	The principal room in a medieval house.
MERLONS	Solid sections of battlements, alternating with void sections; sometimes pierced with slits.
MOTTE	A castle mound of earth or turf. (Eleventh and twelfth centuries.)
PENT	Also pentise, penthouse or lean-to.
PORTCULLIS	An iron-shod wooden grille suspended by chains in grooves in front of a gate.
POSTERN	Smaller or lesser castle gate.
REVETMENT	Retaining wall or facing.
SLIT	Arrow-slit; a narrow opening in a wall for discharge of arrows and admittance of light.
TURNING BRIDGE	A wooden bridge, pivoted on an axle and working like a seesaw, with a counter-poise weight attached to the end nearer the gateway.
WARD	Courtyard or bailey.

Bibliography

The following books and papers are suggested for further reading:

"The Dream of Macsen Wledig" in *The Mabinogion*, translated by T. P. Ellis and John Lloyd (Oxford, 1929), i, 133–50.

M. P. Charlesworth, *The Lost Province* (Gregynog Lectures, 1948), especially Chapter II.

Sir Charles Peers, "Caernarvon Castle" in *Transactions of the Honourable Society of Cymmrodorion*, 1915–16, 1–74.

Sir J. Goronwy Edwards, "Edward I's castle-building in Wales", *Proceedings of the British Academy*, xxxii (1944), 43–52.

A. J. Taylor, "The birth of Edward of Caernarvon and the beginnings of Caernarvon Castle" in *History*, new series, xxxv (1950), 256–61.

A. J. Taylor, "The Date of Caernarvon Castle", *Antiquity*, xxvi (1952), 25–54.

A. J. Taylor, "The King's Works in Wales" in *The History of the King's Works* (HMSO, 1963), 293–408, separately reprinted, 1974.

Royal Commission on Ancient and Historical Monuments in Wales and Monmouthshire, *Inventory of the Ancient Monuments in Caernarvonshire*, ii, (HMSO, 1960), 115–56.

CONVERSION TABLE

1ft	0.3m	30yd	27.4m
5ft	1.5m	35yd	32.0m
10ft	3.0m	40yd	36.6m
15ft	4.6m	45yd	41.1m
20ft	6.1m	50yd	45.7m
25ft	7.6m	100yd	91.4m
30ft	9.1m	200yd	182.9m
35ft	10.7m	300yd	274.3m
40ft	12.2m	400yd	365.8m
45ft	13.7m	500yd	457.2m
50ft	15.2m	1000yd	914.4m
100ft	30.5m		
		1 acre	0.40 hectare
1yd	0.9m	5 acres	2.02 hectares
5yd	4.6m	10 acres	4.05 hectares
10yd	9.1m		
15yd	13.7m	1 mile	1.60km
20yd	18.3m	5 miles	8.04km
25yd	22.9m	10 miles	16.09km

Printed in Scotland by Her Majesty's Stationery Office at HMSO Press, Edinburgh
Dd 289369 K248 2/75 (12090)